This Orchard book belongs to

_____

_____

_____

Ankylosaurus
an-ki-loh-sore-us

Triceratops
try-serra-tops

Iguanodon
ig-wah-noh-don

Brachiosaurus
brak-ee-oh-sore-us

Velociraptor
vel-oss-ee-rap-tor

Plesiosaurus
plee-see-oh-sore-us

Diplodocus
dip-lod-oh-kus

Oviraptor
oh-vee-rap-tor

Pteranodon
ter-an-oh-don

Stegosaurus
steg-oh-sore-us

Tyrannosaurus
tie-ran-oh-sore-us

For Peter — MM

For Henry, Elinor, Ollie and Milly — AA

ORCHARD BOOKS
Carmelite House
50 Victoria Embankment
London EC4Y 0DZ
First published in 2010 by Orchard Books
First published in paperback in 2011
ISBN 978 1 40834 929 8
Text © Margaret Mayo 2010
Illustrations © Alex Ayliffe 2010
The rights of Margaret Mayo to be identified as the author
and of Alex Ayliffe to be identified as illustrator of this work
have been asserted by them in accordance with the
Copyright, Designs and Patents Act, 1988.
A CIP catalogue record for this book
is available from the British Library.
9 10 8
Printed in China
Orchard Books is a division of Hachette Children's Books,
an Hachette UK company.
www.hachette.co.uk

Margaret Mayo & Alex Ayliffe

STOMP, DINOSAUR, STOMP!

ORCHARD

Mighty Tyrannosaurus

loved stomp, **stomp**, **stomping**,

Gigantic legs **striding**, enormous jaws **opening**,

Jagged teeth waiting for guzzle, **guzzling!**

So **stomp**, Tyrannosaurus, **stomp!**

Immense Diplodocus

loved swish, swish, swishing,

Long tail flicking and fast whip, whipping.

Enemy surprising and – **smack!** – scaring.

So **swish**, Diplodocus, **swish!**

Crested Pteranodon

loved glide, glide, gliding,
spreading **wide** wings, circling, rising,

Higher and **higher**, swooping and **soaring**.

So glide, Pteranodon, **glide!**

Fierce Velociraptor

loved hunt, hunt, **hunting**,

In fearsome packs running, **racing**,

Hooked claws ready for quick **pouncing.**

So **hunt**, Velociraptor, **hunt!**

Sleek Plesiosaurus loved zoom, zoom, zooming,

Sturdy paddles swooshing, **flapping,**

Neck lunging, teeth showing – **snatch!** – fish trapping.

So **zoom**, Plesiosaurus, **zoom!**

Tough Ankylosaurus

loved whack, **whack, whacking,**

Tail-club **swinging,** battles winning,

While hiding safely under spikes and armour plating.

So **whack**, Ankylosaurus, **whack!**

Massive Brachiosaurus

loved gulp, gulp, gulping,

Leaves picking, mouth stuffing . . . no chewing! . . . **fast eating,**

Hungry, **hungry** giant . . . **more** food needing.

So **gulp,** Brachiosaurus, **gulp!**

Wrinkly Triceratops

loved charge, **charge, charging,**

Thumpety-thump! Huge feet **pounding,**

Horns jutting and – **wham!** – head-butting.

So charge, Triceratops, **charge!**

Stiff-tailed Iguanodon

loved chomp, chomp, **chomping,**

Tough plants **grabbing,** cutting and **biting,**

Chewing, mashing and noisy **grinding.**

So **chomp,** Iguanodon, **chomp!**

Feathered Oviraptor

loved guard, **guard, guarding,**

Soft sand shaping, snug **nest making,**

Eggs protecting, until – **cric-crac!** – babies **hatching.**

So guard, Oviraptor, **guard!**

Fantastic Stegosaurus

loved stroll, stroll, strolling,

Tiny eyes glaring, spiky tail **waving**,

Showing off big curvy plates . . . and looking quite **amazing!**

So **stroll**, Stegosaurus, **stroll!**

Imagine the creatures in a grand parade –

With no fighting allowed and no one afraid!

Some **plodding**, some **swooping** while others just **romp**,

And Tyrannosaurus leading . . .

STOMP! STOMP! STOMP!

Ankylosaurus
an-ki-loh-sore-us

Triceratops
try-serra-tops

Iguanodon
ig-wah-noh-don

Brachiosaurus
brak-ee-oh-sore-us

Velociraptor
vel-oss-ee-rap-tor

Plesiosaurus
plee-see-oh-sore-us

Diplodocus
dip-lod-oh-kus

Oviraptor
oh-vee-rap-tor

Pteranodon
ter-an-oh-don

Stegosaurus
steg-oh-sore-us

Tyrannosaurus
tie-ran-oh-sore-us